The Secret World of
Lichens
A Young Naturalist's Guide

Troy McMullin
Canadian Museum of Nature

FIREFLY BOOKS

canadian museum of nature
nature
musée canadien de la nature

Copyright information on page 48.

Introduction

Look closely at the trees, rocks and soil in your neighborhood to discover a secret world full of bright colors and interesting shapes that resembles a miniature coral reef. Many of the species you will see are lichens. Lichens grow in virtually every terrestrial environment worldwide, and they have many important functions. They are food, camouflage and nesting material for many animals; they are an important part of the nutrient cycle, particularly by adding nitrogen to soil that can be used by other organisms; and some species that grow on soil prevent erosion. Lichens are also used by humans as dyes, food and medicine. These amazing organisms can even survive in the vacuum and radiation of space (see Elegant Sunburst Lichen on page 21 for more details).

What Are Lichens Anyways?

Lichens are **symbiotic*** organisms, which means they are composed of multiple species working together. They are made up mostly of a primary and sometimes a secondary fungus (80 to 95 percent of the lichen body) and a **photosynthesizing** partner (5 to 20 percent of the lichen body), which is either **algae** or **cyano-bacteria**, or occasionally both! The fungus forms the outer layer, which is called the **thallus**. Algae and/or cyanobacteria live inside the thallus and produce energy (carbohydrates), while other nutrients and minerals are taken in directly from the atmosphere and water that washes over them. Therefore, lichens do not need soil to grow, which is why they can grow on rocks and trees.

Lungwort Lichen (*Lobaria pulmonaria*) is green because it has algae as its primary photosynthesizing partner.

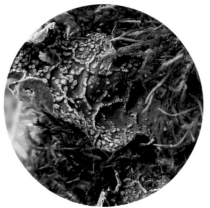

Netted Lungwort Lichen (*Lobaria anomala*), growing with a moss, is brown because it has cyanobacteria as its primary photosynthesizing partner.

*Words that are **bolded** are defined in the glossary on page 47.

What Do Lichens Look Like?

There are three main lichen forms. The first is **crustose**, which grows directly into a **substrate** (e.g., trees, rocks or soil), so this form has no visible lower surface. The second is **foliose**, which resembles leaves (or foliage), with distinct upper and lower surfaces that are typically different colors. The third form is **fruticose**, which has long and narrow branches that appear bush-like or hairy. The surface of a fruticose lichen is usually the same on all sides.

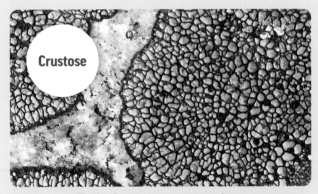

Copper Patch Lichen (*Sporastatia testudinea*) is a crustose lichen that grows on rocks in arctic and alpine environments.

Rippled Ring Lichen (*Arctoparmelia separata*) is an arctic foliose lichen that grows on soil and rocks.

Star-Tipped Reindeer Lichen (*Cladonia stellaris*) is a bush-like fruticose lichen that grows on soil. It is Canada's unofficial national lichen.

Horsehair Lichen (*Bryoria* spp.) is brown and Old Man's Beard (*Usnea* spp.) is yellowish green. These are hair-like fruticose species growing on the branches of a conifer tree. See Horsehair Lichen on page 28 for a close-up example.

Lichen Reproduction and Structure

The illustration on the right is a side view showing the internal structures of a typical foliose lichen. On the top are the modes of reproduction, both vegetative (e.g., soredia and isidia) and sexual (e.g., **apothecia**). Soredia are produced from within the lichen and include small amounts of algae or cyanobacteria and fungi; they usually look like fine soft powder. Isidia also contain algae and fungi, but they grow on the surface and break off; they usually look hard and rough. Soredia and isidia will form a new lichen if they reach a suitable environment. They are moved to new locations by animals, rain and wind.

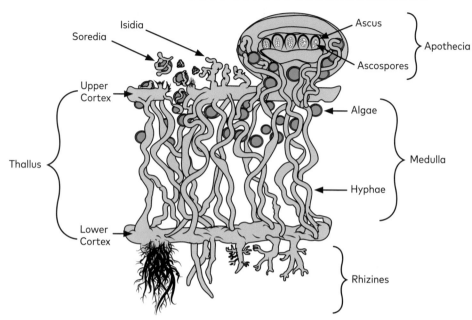

The apothecia, which are also called **fruiting bodies**, produce **ascospores** within them. As the ascospores develop, pressure builds and they are finally ejected into the air. They are also transported by animals, rain and wind. For a new lichen to form, the ascospores need to land in a suitable environment, but they also need to find a photo-synthesizing partner (algae or cyanobacteria). Sometimes the ascospores will land on other lichens, germinate and then use the photosynthesizing partner of the lichen that they landed on. Lichens usually only reproduce using one mode, either with soredia, isidia or a fruiting body like apothecia.

In the middle, there is an upper and lower **cortex** composed of dense fungi. Between the cortices are loose fungi, the **medulla**, where the algae or cyanobacteria typically live. They usually form a thin layer just below the upper cortex. This is because the upper cortex becomes more transparent when wet to allow light to reach the photosynthesizing partner inside. When lichens are wet, they usually become greener because the algal layer is visible (see Smooth Lungwort Lichen on the opposite page) or darker for those with cyanobacteria (see Yellow Specklebelly Lichen on the opposite page).

On the bottom, below the lower cortex, foliose lichens often produce **rhizines**. Rhizines have several forms (some of them are illustrated in the diagram). Although rhizines look like roots, they are only attachment structures that keep lichens connected to their substrates (e.g., rocks, trees or soil).

The algae inside Smooth Lungwort Lichen (*Ricasolia quercizans*) become more visible when it is wet. These photos show what this lichen looks like when it is dry (left) and wet (right).

The cyanobacteria inside Yellow Specklebelly Lichen (*Pseudocyphellaria holarctica*) become more visible when it is wet. These photos show what this lichen looks like when it is dry (left) and wet (right).

Lichen Growth, Age and Fossils

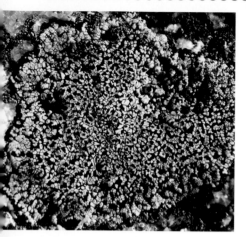

Yellow Map Lichen (*Rhizocarpon geographicum*) is the oldest-known lichen at about 8,600 years old.

How quickly lichens grow depends on many environmental variables. Their metabolism (the chemical reactions in cells that change food into energy) is regulated by water availability. In other words, the more light they receive while they are wet, the faster they grow. Other variables affecting their growth include what they are growing on (substrate), tempera-ture, snow depth, air pollution and acid rain.

On average, fruticose lichens are the fastest-growing form (1.5 to 7 millimeters per year), followed by foliose lichens (0.5 to 5.5 millimeters per year). Crustose lichens are the slowest growing (0.5 to 3 millimeters per year). However, there are more extreme examples, such as an unknown foliose lichen with cyano-bacteria in the Te Urewera protected area in New Zealand, which grew at a rate of 27 millimeters per year!

The oldest lichens grow in arctic-alpine environments. They can live to be over 1,000 years old, and the oldest-known individual is a Yellow Map Lichen (*Rhizocarpon geographicum*) that is estimated to be about 8,600 years old. This makes lichens one of the oldest-living organisms on Earth!

Lichens have also been around for a long time. The oldest fossils that resemble lichens are about 600 million years old from Southern China and about 480 million years old from Scotland, but it is unclear what these fossils actually were. Fossils clearly related to modern lichens are known from the Cretaceous period (145 to 66 million years ago) — when dinosaurs walked the Earth — but most older lichen fossils are from the Paleogene period (66 to 23 million years ago) and are preserved in amber.

How Are Lichens Used?

People use lichens in many ways throughout the world, such as for food, medicine, poison, dyes and monitoring air pollution. Their use often involves some of the over 1,000 chemicals lichens produce, which give many species their spectacular colors. One of the more common lichen chemicals that is used medicinally is usnic acid, which has antibacterial properties. Most

Oakmoss Lichen (*Evernia prunastri*) is added to bread in Egypt. It is also a commercially important perfume fixative in Europe because it contributes to the fragrance and helps make the scent last longer.

lichens that contain usnic acid have a yellowish-green color. Several species in this book contain usnic acid, including Oakmoss Lichen (opposite page), Arctic Kidney Lichen (page 12), Arctic Oakmoss Lichen (page 13), Methuselah's Beard Lichen (page 34) and Orange Rock-Posy (page 36).

A very small number of lichens are poisonous, but one of the more toxic chemicals that they can produce is vulpinic acid. Lichens with this chemical are bright yellow, such as Brown-Eyed Wolf Lichen (*Letharia columbiana*) and Wolf Lichen (*Letharia vulpina*), which has been used to poison foxes and wolves in Scandinavia. These species also produce a bright yellow dye.

It is speculated that lichen dyes were first used in China about 4,000 years ago. The oldest-known lichen dye recipe was written about 1,800 years ago in Greece. Today, artists and weavers still use lichen dyes, and in Scotland some Harris Tweeds, a type of cloth made out of wool, are still dyed with Crottle Lichen (*Parmelia saxatilis*) and Smoky Crottle Lichen (*Parmelia omphalodes*).

Lichens are also used as indicators of air pollution. Since lichens obtain minerals and nutrients directly from the atmosphere, they also take in pollutants from the air.

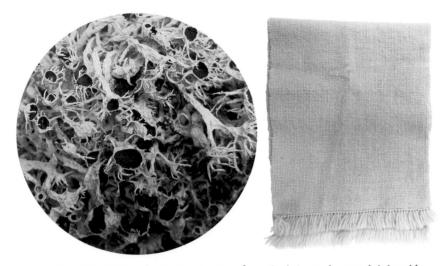

Brown-Eyed Wolf Lichen (*Letharia columbiana*), on the left, produces vulpinic acid, which makes it bright yellow. It is used to make a bright yellow dye. This yellow scarf was dyed with Wolf Lichen (*Letharia vulpina*), which has the same chemical as Brown-Eyed Wolf Lichen, vulpinic acid.

Smooth Rock Tripe Lichen (*Umbilicaria mammulata*), on the left, produces gyrophoric acid and was used to dye this purple scarf.

This Ilia Underwing (*Calocala ilia*) moth caterpillar in Alabama, USA, uses lichen for camouflage. It is able to blend in with many common lichens, including the Tube Lichens (*Hypogymnia* spp.), Shield Lichens (*Parmelia* spp.), Ruffled Lichens (*Parmotrema* spp.) and Speckled Shield Lichens (*Punctelia* spp.).

The eggs of the American Golden Plover (*Pluvialis dominica*) sit in a nest built with Whiteworm Lichen (*Thamnolia vermicularis*). For more information about Whiteworm Lichen see page 44.

Some lichens are more sensitive to air pollution than others, and they will disappear first if pollutants are present. An example of a lichen that is sensitive to air pollution is Lungwort Lichen on page 31. It is one of the lichens used to monitor air quality at Kejimkujik National Park and National Historic Site in Nova Scotia, Canada.

Animals also use lichens in a variety of ways. Some animals, such as birds and squirrels, use lichens as nesting material. Others, mainly insects, use lichens as camouflage. Many animals also eat lichens, including Caribou/Reindeer, which often rely on them in the winter months more than any other food source.

This bag of dyed Star-Tipped Reindeer Lichen (*Cladonia stellaris*), which you can see up close on page 3, is used for things like trees on architecture models and model train sets.

True Iceland Lichen (*Cetraria islandica*) is used in this tea and candy.

A baby Caribou/Reindeer (*Rangifer tarandus*) munches on some Reindeer Lichen (*Cladonia* sp.). Caribou and Reindeer are different names for the same species. In North America, they are called Caribou and in Asia and Europe they are called Reindeer.

Revealing the Secret World of Lichens

There are approximately 20,000 lichens described worldwide. In this book, you can learn about 38 interesting and beautiful species that are found from the Arctic to the tropics. Once you get an eye for lichens, you will start seeing them everywhere. That is when you know their secret world has been revealed!

Looking for Lichens

Lichens can grow just about anywhere. In the forest, you will find them on rocks, soil and trees. In dark forests (those with a dense canopy), larger lichens often grow in the canopy where there is more light. Therefore, fallen branches are a good place to look for lichens. Other good places to look for lichens are on old wooden fences in fields, rock outcrops and cliffs in forests, large boulders in fields and shoreline rocks (freshwater and saltwater).

In cities, one of the best places to look is on big trees (in your yard or at the park). Several species also grow on concrete, like roadside curbs, but they are usually very small.

Many lichens are small and getting a good look at their structures is difficult without a magnifying glass or hand lens.

Lichens are slow growing, and many species are rare, so it is best not to collect them or remove them from their environment. Instead, take a picture of your discovery and write down where it was growing (location), what it was growing on (substrate) and when you observed it (date). This information can be used to help you identify a lichen species using field guides or online apps like iNaturalist (inaturalist.org).

Alpine Bloodspot Lichen   (*Ophioparma ventosa*) [left]
Orange Boulder Lichen   (*Porpidia flavicunda*) [right]

These two brightly colored crustose lichens are common on rocks in arctic-alpine environments in Asia, Europe, North America and South America. The fruiting bodies (apothecia) look like spots, and each one is 1 to 2.5 millimeters wide, though they can occasionally grow up to 5 millimeters wide. Alpine Bloodspot Lichen is used to make a purplish-red dye.

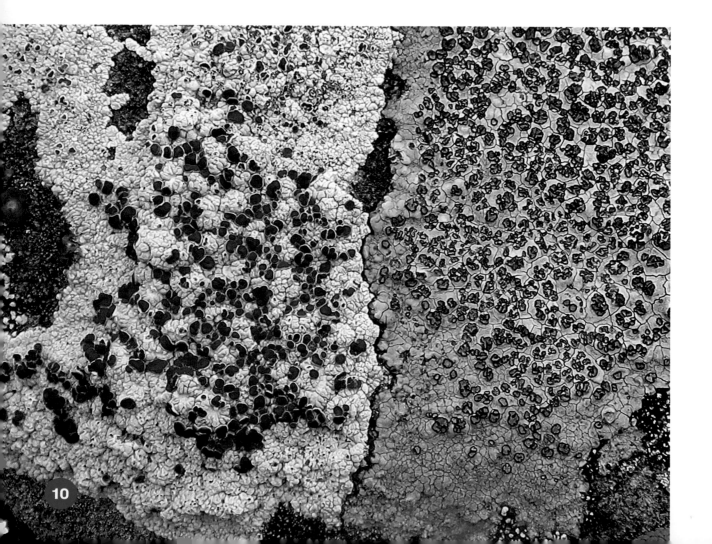

Arctic Finger Lichen (*Dactylina arctica*)

This inflated-looking fruticose lichen is common in arctic-alpine regions throughout Asia, Europe and North America. It is hollow with thin walls (see inset photo) and grows on soil. The largest stalks are up to 7 centimeters tall. Another common name for this species is Dead Man's Fingers.

Arctic Kidney Lichen *(Nephroma arcticum)*

This foliose lichen is frequent on soil in arctic-alpine and subarctic-subalpine conditions throughout Asia, Europe and North America. Its bright orange fruiting bodies (apothecia) are shaped like kidneys, hence its name. Arctic Kidney Lichen has two photosynthesizing partners: algae where it is green, and cyanobacteria, which can be seen in the small dark patches on the **lobe** in the lower right-hand corner (circled). The lobes are 2 to 5 centimeters wide.

Arctic Oakmoss Lichen (*Evernia perfragilis*)

Arctic Oakmoss Lichen lives on basic soil (soil with a high pH) in arctic-alpine regions throughout Asia, Europe and North America. It is somewhat common in North America and only known to exist in the Alps in Europe. This fruticose lichen is 2 to 5 centimeters tall and looks similar to Reindeer Lichens, but it is not one. Arctic Oakmoss Lichen is solid, and it has a hard, shiny outer layer called a cortex. Reindeer Lichens are hollow and have no cortex, so under a microscope they look dull and webby.

Arctic Tumbleweed Lichen (*Masonhalea richardsonii*)

Unlike most lichens, which are anchored down, this species rolls freely like a tumbleweed. It is a showy fruticose lichen that lives in arctic-alpine conditions in eastern Russia and northern parts of western North America, where it is fairly common. Its branches are 2 to 7 millimeters wide. Its scientific name, *Masonhalea richardsonii*, honours Mason Hale, a lichenologist at the Smithsonian Institution in the later part of the 20th century, and Sir John Richardson, a naval surgeon, naturalist and Arctic explorer in the early part of the 19th century.

Blushing Rock Tripe Lichen (*Umbilicaria virginis*)

Like all species in the genus *Umbilicaria*, Blushing Rock Tripe Lichen is foliose and connected to rocks by a single point in the middle called an **umbilicus**. It is somewhat common in arctic-alpine regions in Asia, Australasia, Europe and North America. Most individuals are 1.5 to 5 centimeters in diameter but can occasionally be up to 20 centimeters wide. The round, black growths on the upper surface are the fruiting bodies (apothecia). The lower surface is tan to pink and has numerous hair-like growths called rhizines.

Scientific names (the italicized names in brackets throughout this book) are the official names given to species. The genus is the first part, and the species is the second. Genera and species are written in either Greek or Latin and are universally used. Common names (for instance, Blushing Rock Tripe Lichen) are not as official, and they can be different in different parts of the world.

Christmas Lichen (*Herpothallon rubrocinctum*)

This striking crustose lichen is common on trees from the southeastern United States to Argentina. It grows several centimeters in diameter. Its festive name is based on its color. The bright red pigment is called chiodectonic acid. Although the individual here is only red and white, it can also develop a green coloration as it matures. It has been used to make a red dye in South America.

Common Freckle Pelt Lichen (*Peltigera aphthosa*)

Individuals of this relatively large foliose lichen can be up to 20 centimeters wide. It is a frequent species in several forest types and arctic-alpine environments throughout Asia, Australasia, Europe and North America. It grows on mossy soil, rocks and tree bases and has two photosynthesizing partners. The green areas have algae, and the dark "freckles" are filled with cyanobacteria.

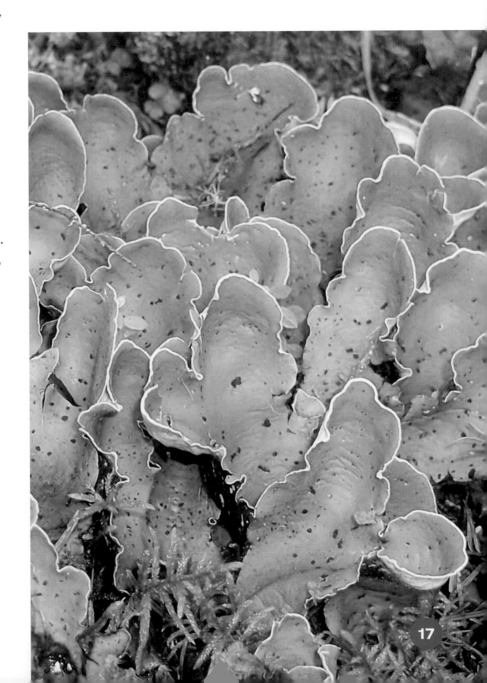

Concentric Ring Lichen (*Arctoparmelia centrifuga*)

This common foliose lichen grows on rocks in arctic-alpine and subarctic-subalpine regions throughout Asia, Europe and North America. The outer edge is where new growth occurs. The older parts of this lichen die off and new growth takes their place, which creates distinctive concentric rings that can be up to a meter wide.

"Concentric" means having the same center, like the rings of a target or those of the Concentric Ring Lichen.

Devil's Matchstick Lichen (*Pilophorus acicularis*)

This distinctive and showy fruticose lichen grows on rocks and is common in western North America. There are also a few reports of it from eastern Asia. It is a pioneer species that often grows on newly exposed rocks. The stalks are 5 to 25 millimeters tall. The black tips are the fruiting bodies (apothecia). Devil's Matchstick Lichen contains two photosynthesizing partners: algae where it is green, and cyanobacteria in pink to brown lumps on the rock surface, which are not visible in the picture.

Dimpled Lungwort Lichen (*Lobaria anthraspis*)

Individuals of this large foliose lichen are usually up to 20 centimeters wide, but they can occasionally grow up to 40 centimeters across. The photosynthesizing partner in Dimpled Lungwort Lichen is cyanobacteria, which gives it a dark color. This species of lichen grows throughout the west coast of North America on trees of all kinds and mossy rocks. It prefers mature forests with high humidity.

Elegant Sunburst Lichen (*Rusavskia elegans*)

This bright orange foliose lichen is common on rocks in Africa, Antarctica, Asia, Australasia, Europe, North America and South America. It is particularly abundant in arctic-alpine habitats and on maritime coastal rocks. It is also frequently found on rocks regularly fertilized by bird and mammal droppings. As a result, the movements of some animals can be tracked by the presence of this species. Most individuals are up to 5 centimeters in diameter, but they can grow up to 10 centimeters wide.

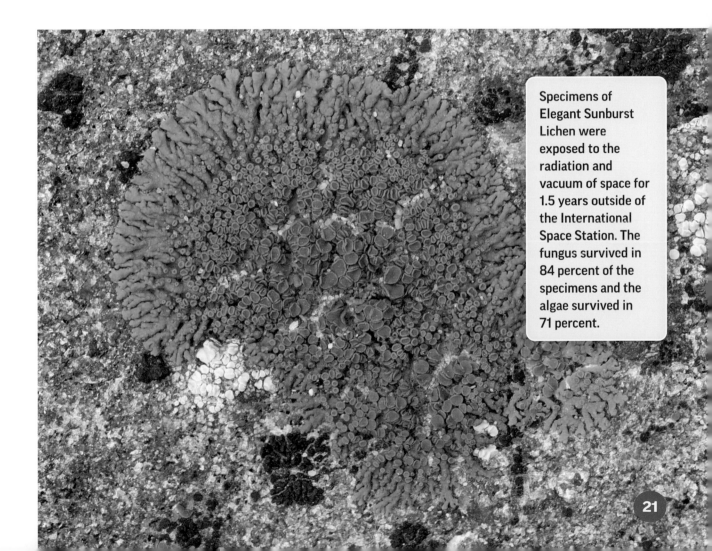

Specimens of Elegant Sunburst Lichen were exposed to the radiation and vacuum of space for 1.5 years outside of the International Space Station. The fungus survived in 84 percent of the specimens and the algae survived in 71 percent.

Fairy Puke Lichen (*Icmadophila ericetorum*)

This brightly colored crustose lichen overgrows mosses, rotting wood and peat. It is somewhat common in a wide range of habitats in Africa, Asia, Australasia, Europe and North America. The fruiting bodies (apothecia) can grow up to 4 millimeters in diameter and are bright pink, which makes them hard to miss.

Fishnet Cladonia Lichen (*Cladonia boryi*)

Fishnet Cladonia Lichen is a frequent coastal fruticose lichen in eastern North America. Its distinctive stalks are up to 9 centimeters tall and heavily perforated (full of holes), like a fishnet.

Flowering Fringe Lichen (*Heterodermia echinata*)

The long **cilia** along the edges of the Flowering Fringe Lichen make it look hairy, and its form is between foliose (because it has distinct upper and lower surfaces) and fruticose (because it has long narrow lobes). It typically grows on tree branches in forested habitats. The grayish-blue structures at the ends of the lobes are the fruiting bodies (apothecia). The lobes themselves are 1 to 3 millimeters across. Flowering Fringe Lichen grows from the southeastern United States to Central America.

Frosted Finger Lichen (*Dactylina ramulosa*)

This distinctive fruticose lichen is frequent on the soil in arctic-alpine habitats throughout Asia, Europe and North America. It grows up to 4 centimeters tall. The areas that are white or frosty looking are from the chemicals inside crystalizing on the surface.

Fruiting Honeycomb Lichen (*Hypogymnia lophyrea*)

This coastal foliose lichen is frequent on conifer trees in northwestern North America. It grows up to 1.5 centimeters wide and has distinctive pits on the lower surface that resemble a honeycomb, which its name is based on (see inset photo).

Green Specklebelly Lichen (*Crocodia aurata*)

Green Specklebelly Lichen is an eye-catching foliose lichen that is frequent at scattered locations in temperate and tropical regions throughout Africa, Asia, Australasia, Europe, North America and South America. Its lobes are 0.5 to 1 centimeter wide, the medulla is yellow, and there are bright yellow speckles on the lower surface, or belly (see inset photo), which the "specklebelly" part of its name is based on.

Horsehair Lichen (*Bryoria trichodes*)

There are many types of hair-like lichens, such as Old Man's Beard (*Usnea* spp.) and Witch's Hair (*Alectoria* spp.). Horsehair Lichen is distinguished by its fine, brown fruticose branches, which can grow up to 15 centimeters long. It is most abundant in boreal forests in North America, but it also occurs in Europe and Japan. Flying squirrels use Horsehair Lichen to build their nests.

Lichen Agaric (*Lichenomphalia umbellifera*)

Lichen Agaric is one of the few lichens with gilled fruiting bodies. It is common throughout Asia, Europe and North America in forest and arctic-alpine environments and can be found on soil and rotting wood. The part of this lichen with algae is the dark green layer at the base of the fruiting bodies. This species has two forms, the crustose base (circled) and the fruticose fruiting bodies.

Limestone Sunshine Lichen (*Vulpicida tilesii*)

This brilliant-yellow foliose lichen is frequent in arctic-alpine regions throughout Asia, Europe and North America. It only grows on soil that is basic (has a high pH), like limestone, which its name is based on. The lobes are 0.5 to 4 millimeters wide and contain vulpinic acid, which can be used to make a bright yellow dye (see Brown-Eyed Wolf Lichen and Wolf Lichen on page 7 for more information about the use of vulpinic acid).

Lungwort Lichen (*Lobaria pulmonaria*)

This large leafy foliose lichen prefers to live in old forests on trees and occasionally mossy rocks. It is widespread in parts of Africa, Asia, Europe and North America. The lobes are up to 7 centimeters long and their ridges and depressions resemble the surface of the inside of lungs. Lungwort Lichen is used to make a light orange-brown dye. In Europe, this species is rare and declining.

Maritime Reindeer Lichen (*Cladonia portentosa* ssp. *pacifica*)

This heavily branched fruticose lichen is one of many species of Reindeer Lichen, which, as a group, are an important food source for Caribou/Reindeer, particularly in the winter months. Other species of Reindeer Lichen are more widespread, but Maritime Reindeer Lichen is restricted mostly to coastal environments in western North America. Most individuals grow up to 7 centimeters tall.

Mealy Pixie-Cup Lichen (*Cladonia chlorophaea*)

There are many species of Pixie-Cup Lichen that look almost identical to Mealy Pixie-Cup Lichen, but they produce different chemicals. To determine the species, tests are needed to find out which chemicals are present. Mealy Pixie-Cup Lichen is common throughout Antarctica, Asia, Australasia, Europe, North America and South America and can be found on soil, wood and bark. It actually has two forms: the small leaflets (circled) are foliose, and the stalks with cups are fruticose. It is usually considered fruticose because the stalks are larger and more conspicuous.

Methuselah's Beard Lichen (*Usnea longissima*)

Methuselah's Beard Lichen grows in single strands up to 3 meters long. Each strand has a central branch with numerous small side branches. It is thought to have been used as the first Christmas tree tinsel in Northern Europe. This long fruticose lichen is sensitive to air pollution and has been declining throughout its range. It lives in Asia, Europe and North America.

Mottled Tube Lichen (*Hypogymnia inactiva*)

Mottled Tube Lichen lives in western North America. It is a showy hollow foliose species that grows on the trunks and branches of conifer trees. The fruiting bodies (apothecia) are the brown circular structures. This species is common west of the Cascade Mountains, which extend from southern British Columbia to northern California.

Orange Rock-Posy Lichen (*Rhizoplaca chrysoleuca*)

This foliose lichen grows on rocks and is connected by a single attachment point in the middle, which is called an umbilicus. The lichen grows up to 3 centimeters in diameter. The orange structures are the fruiting bodies (apothecia). Orange Rock-Posy Lichen is widespread in Asia, Europe and North America in arctic-alpine and subarctic-subalpine environments.

Pink Bull's-Eye Lichen (*Placopsis lambii*)

This crustose lichen grows on exposed rocks in Africa, Australasia, Europe, North America and South America. It has two photosynthesizing partners: the whitish areas are where the algae live, and the pink parts contain cyanobacteria. Individuals grow up to 5 centimeters in diameter.

Polypore Stubble Lichen (*Chaenotheca obscura*)

This tiny lichen is less than 1.5 millimeters tall and lives in a very specific place. It only grows on Purplepore Bracket (*Trichaptum abietinum*), a polypore fungus found on dead conifer trees. It is common but rarely reported because it is often overlooked due to its small size. The dark stalks are the fruticose fruiting bodies of the lichen, and the whitish part at the bottom is the polypore fungus. Polypore Stubble Lichen is known to live in boreal and temperate forests in Europe and North America. It likely occurs in Asia and possibly other regions, but it has not yet been reported.

Puckered Rocktripe Lichen (*Umbilicaria lyngei*)

This foliose lichen lives in arctic-alpine habitats in Asia, Europe and North America. It is attached to rocks by a single point in the middle, called an umbilicus (the genus is named after the umbilicus). The lower surface of Puckered Rocktripe Lichen is black and has a soot-like texture. It grows up to 5 centimeters in diameter.

Quill Lichen (*Cladonia amaurocraea*)

This showy fruticose lichen is common in arctic-alpine and subarctic-subalpine environments in Asia, Europe and North America. It grows up to 12 centimeters tall and is eaten by Caribou/Reindeer.

Sea-Storm Lichen (*Cetrelia olivetorum*)

The uncommon foliose Sea-Storm Lichen is sensitive and tends to grow on trees and rocks in older forests, gorges and river valleys. There are several species in the genus *Cetrelia* that look very similar, but they all produce different chemicals. Sea-Storm Lichen is the only one that produces olivetoric acid, which its scientific name is based on. Individuals grow up to 20 centimeters wide. It lives in Asia, Australasia, Europe, North America and South America.

Toy Soldiers Lichen (*Cladonia bellidiflora*)

The bright red fruiting bodies (apothecia) and numerous small leaflets on the stalks make Toy Soldiers Lichen a striking fruticose species. It is common in arctic-alpine and subarctic-subalpine environments in Antarctica, Asia, Australasia, Europe, North America and South America. The stalks grow up to 5 centimeters tall.

Volcano Lichen (*Coccotrema maritimum*)

This distinctive crustose lichen grows in northwestern North America on coastal rocks that are sprayed by ocean waves. The round structures, each with a single depression, are the fruiting bodies (apothecia), which look like small volcanoes. The fruiting bodies grow up to 1.5 millimeters wide.

Whiteworm Lichen (*Thamnolia vermicularis*)

This fruticose lichen is very abundant in arctic-alpine regions in Asia, Australasia, Europe and North America. The American Golden Plover (*Pluvialis dominica*) uses Whiteworm Lichen to build its nest (you can see this on page 8). Branches can grow up to 10 centimeters long. It is the unofficial territorial lichen of Nunavut, Canada.

Wrinkled Shingle Lichen (*Pannaria lurida*)

Wrinkled Shingle Lichen is dark colored because the photosynthesizing partner is cyanobacteria. The dark-orange structures are the fruiting bodies (apothecia). The specimen in the photo is wet. When dry, this foliose lichen is light gray, like the color of the lobe tips in the photo, and more wrinkled, which its common name is based on. Individuals can grow up to 9 centimeters wide, typically on tree trunks. It is a rare species that is listed as "threatened" by the federal Species at Risk Act in Canada.

A "threatened" species listed on Canada's Species at Risk Act means "a wildlife species that is likely to become an endangered species if nothing is done to reverse the factors leading to its extirpation or extinction."

Yellow Collar Stubble Lichen (*Calicium trabinellum*)

It might be difficult to see this fruticose lichen with the naked eye because it is less than 1 millimeter tall. Although Yellow Collar Stubble Lichen can occur in younger forests, most species of stubble lichens prefer to live in old-growth forests. This species lives on the bark and wood of live and dead trees in Africa, Asia, Australasia and North America. The dark stalk is the fruiting body, and the body of the lichen is within the wood and not visible. The algae live in the body of the lichen. The yellow collar contains vulpinic acid (see Brown-Eyed Wolf Lichen and Wolf Lichen on page 7 for more information about vulpinic acid).

Glossary

Alga (plural = algae): A group of **photosynthetic** (containing chlorophyll) organisms with a nucleus that lack roots, stems, leaves or multicellular reproductive structures. They are the most common **photosynthesizing** partners in lichens.

Apothecium (plural = apothecia): Reproductive structures where fungal **ascospores** are produced.

Ascospore: A **spore** formed within an **ascus**.

Ascus (plural = asci): A sac-like structure in which ascospores are sexually produced.

Cilium (plural = cilia): A slender, hair-like growth typically on the margin of thalli or apothecia.

Cortex (plural = cortices): The protective outermost layer of the **thallus**; composed of dense fungal filaments called hyphae.

Crustose: A crust-like lichen growth form that grows tightly to its **substrate** across the entire lower surface. As a result, this form does not have a visible lower surface.

Cyanobacteria: A group of chlorophyll-containing **photosynthetic** bacteria. Lichens with cyanobacteria as their primary **photosynthesizing** partner are generally black, dark gray or dark brown.

Foliose: A leaf-like lichen growth form, which typically has distinct upper and lower surfaces.

Fruiting body: The sexual, **spore**-producing structure of a lichen.

Fruticose: A bush-like or hairy lichen growth form, typically without distinct upper and lower surfaces.

Lobe: A rounded or elliptical projection of the **thallus** margin. In lichens, lobe typically refers to the leaf-like projections on **foliose** lichens, but occasionally **crustose** lichens have lobes as well (Pink Bull's-Eye Lichen on page 37 is an example of a crustose lichen with small lobes).

Medulla: A loose layer of interwoven fungal strands (hyphae) in the interior of the **thallus**, beneath the **cortex**. Most often the medulla is white, but occasionally it is orange or yellow.

Photosynthesis: The process of using energy from sunlight to convert water and carbon dioxide into sugars (carbohydrates).

Rhizine: A root-like structure formed on the lower surface of lichens that anchors them to their **substrates**. Rhizines of different species can vary in length, width and degree of branching.

Spore: A microscopic, sexual propagule capable of reproducing the fungus only. Spores can vary in size, shape and number of cells.

Substrate: The surface that something (e.g., a lichen) is growing on (e.g., soil, wood, bark or rock).

Symbiotic: Living in or relating to **symbiosis**.

Symbiosis: A prolonged close relationship between two or more unrelated organisms. In lichens, the symbiosis is between fungi and one or more **photosynthesizing** partners.

Thallus (plural = thalli): The vegetative body of a lichen.

Umbilicus: A short, thick, central attachment structure or holdfast occurring in some lichens, including *Rhizoplaca* and *Umbilicaria*.

For Maeve

A FIREFLY BOOK

Published by Firefly Books Ltd. 2022
Copyright © 2022 Firefly Books Ltd.
Copyright © 2022 Canadian Museum of Nature
Text by R. Troy McMullin, PhD, Research Scientist, Lichenology, Canadian Museum of Nature
Photographs by R. Troy McMullin, except as listed below

FIRST PRINTING

Library of Congress Control Number: 2022932514

Library and Archives Canada Cataloguing in Publication

Title: The secret world of lichens : a young naturalist's guide / Troy McMullin ; Canadian Museum of Nature.
Names: McMullin, Troy, author. | Canadian Museum of Nature, issuing body.
Identifiers: Canadiana 20220169632 | ISBN 9780228103998 (hardcover) | ISBN 9780228103981 (softcover)
Subjects: LCSH: Lichens—Juvenile literature. | LCSH: Lichens—Identification—Juvenile literature.
Classification: LCC QK583 .M36 2022 | DDC j579.7—dc23

Published in the United States by
Firefly Books (U.S.) Inc.
P.O. Box 1338, Ellicott Station
Buffalo, New York 14205

Published in Canada by
Firefly Books Ltd.
50 Staples Avenue, Unit 1
Richmond Hill, Ontario L4B 0A7

Cover and interior design: Gareth Lind, Lind Design
Printed in China

Canada

We acknowledge the financial support of the Government of Canada.

Additional Photo Credits

Back cover (author photo): Paul Sokoloff

Page 4 (illustration): George A. Walker

Page 8 (American Golden Plover nest): Wikimedia Commons/MeegsC (CC-BY-SA 2.5)

Page 8 (Caribou/Reindeer): iStock/S_Z